W9-CHX-449

BIOGRAPHIES OF DIVERSE HEROES

KETANJI BROWN JACKSON

STEPHANIE GASTON

TABLE OF CONTENTS

A Crabtree Seedlings Book

CRABTREE
Publishing Company
www.crabtreebooks.com

School-to-Home Support for Caregivers and Teachers

This book helps children grow by letting them practice reading. Here are a few guiding questions to help the reader with building his or her comprehension skills. Possible answers appear here in red.

Before Reading:
• What do I think this book is about?
  • *I think this book is about Ketanji Brown Jackson.*
  • *I think this book is about the first Black woman to be confirmed to the United States Supreme Court.*

• What do I want to learn about this topic?
  • *I want to learn more about the women who have served on the Supreme Court.*
  • *I want to learn more about other Black Americans who have served on the Supreme Court.*

During Reading:
• I wonder why...
  • *I wonder why a Black woman has never been nominated to the Supreme Court before 2022.*
  • *I wonder why there are so few women nominated to the Supreme Court.*

• What have I learned so far?
  • *I have learned that Ketanji Brown Jackson and Jeff Bezos both went to Miami Palmetto Senior High School in Miami.*
  • *I have learned that Ketanji Brown Jackson graduated with honors from both Harvard University and Harvard Law School.*

After Reading:
• What details did I learn about this topic?
  • *I have learned that Ketanji Brown Jackson's father was the chief attorney for the Miami-Dade County School Board.*
  • *I have learned that Jackson's mother was the principal at the New World School of the Arts.*

• Read the book again and look for the glossary words.
  • *I see the words **Supreme Court** on page 3 and the word **confirmed** on page 15. The other glossary words are found on page 22.*

KETANJI BROWN JACKSON

Ketanji Brown Jackson is the first Black woman **nominated** to the United States **Supreme Court**.

Judge Jackson was born in Washington, D.C., on September 14, 1970.

She later grew up in Miami, Florida, where she was an excellent student.

Jackson was the student body president of Miami Palmetto Senior High School in 1988.

Jeff Bezos, the founder of Amazon, also attended Miami Palmetto Senior High School.

SCHOOL

Jackson's father was the chief **attorney** for the Miami-Dade County School Board.

Jackson's father was a school teacher before becoming a lawyer. Her love for the law came from her father.

*Johnny and Ellery Brown supporting their daughter during her Supreme Court **confirmation**.*

Her mother served as school principal at the New World School of the Arts.

Jackson graduated with honors from both Harvard University and Harvard Law School.

In the beginning of her career, Jackson was a **clerk** for U.S. Supreme Court Justice Stephen Breyer.

Justice Breyer retiring from the Supreme Court made way for Jackson's nomination.

President Obama nominated Jackson to be a judge for the U.S. District Court for the District of Columbia in 2012.

She was **confirmed** as a circuit court judge in 2013.

Jackson was one of the first people President Biden nominated to be a judge.

She was confirmed to the U.S. Court of Appeals for the D.C. Circuit in 2021.

Sandra Day O'Connor was the first woman to serve on the Supreme Court from 1981 to 2006.

Sonia Sotomayor is the first **Hispanic** woman to serve on the Supreme Court.

On February 25, 2022, President Joe Biden nominated Jackson to become the next Associate Judge of the U.S. Supreme Court.

On April 7, 2022, Jackson's historic nomination was confirmed by the Senate. She is now the first Black woman to serve on the Supreme Court.

Glossary

attorney (uh-tur-nee): A person whose job is to represent people in court

clerk (klurk): An attorney who works as an assistant to a judge

confirmation (kon-fer-mey-shun): The event when it is formally announced that someone has earned a position

confirmed (kuhn-furmd): To be formally announced as having earned a position

Hispanic (hi-span-ik): Relating to Spanish-speaking countries, especially those of Latin America

nominated (nom-uh-neyt-id): To be officially named as someone in the running during an election

Supreme Court (suh-preem kawrt): The highest court in a country or state

Index

"Be open to new ideas and experiences because you'll never know when someone else will have an interesting thought or when a new door will open to take you on the journey of your dreams."

—Ketanji Brown Jackson

About the Author

Stephanie Gaston is a content producer for CNN and a screenwriter. She spent more than a decade working for the FOX and ABC affiliates in Miami, Florida, before joining the ranks at CNN in 2015, ahead of an unprecedented election cycle. Stephanie is a first-generation Haitian American who grew up in Fort Lauderdale, Florida, a diverse community with Latin and Caribbean influences. Throughout her career in journalism, Stephanie has covered major stories including presidential inaugurations, natural disasters, and royal weddings. Stephanie is a dog lover, movie buff, fitness enthusiast, and most importantly, a proud mom.

BIOGRAPHIES OF DIVERSE HEROES

KETANJI BROWN JACKSON

Written by: Stephanie Gaston
Designed by: Under the Oaks Media
Proofreader: Petrice Custance

Photographs: White House: cover, p. 13, 18, 19; Rose Lincoln: p. 3; Sean Pavone: p. 5; Felix Miziaznikov; lev cadin: p. 7; Los Angeles Times: p. 9; PT Gui: p. 10; Alexf: p. 11; Christopher Halloran: p. 14; H2rty: p. 15; Adam Schultz: p. 20; Cameron Smith: p. 21

Crabtree Publishing Company

www.crabtreebooks.com   1-800-387-7650

Printed in the U.S.A./072022/CG20220201

Published in Canada
Crabtree Publishing
616 Welland Ave.
St. Catharines, Ontario
L2M 5V6

Published in the United States
Crabtree Publishing
347 Fifth Ave
Suite 1402-145
New York, NY 10016

Library and Archives Canada Cataloguing in Publication
Available at the Library and Archives Canada

Library of Congress Cataloging-in-Publication Data
Available at the Library of Congress

Hardcover: 978-1-0396-8793-6
Ebook (pdf): 978-1-0396-8794-3
Read-along: 978-1-0396-8797-4

Paperback: 978-1-0396-8792-9
Epub: 978-1-0396-8796-7
Audio book: 978-1-0396-8795-0